ALL THINGS NEW

Peter Jeffery

G000240658

BRYNTIRION PRESS

© Peter Jeffery, 1976
First published 1976
Reprinted 1977, 1979, 1982
Second edition 1984
Reprinted 1986, 1988, 1991, 1993, 1999, 2003

ISBN 1 85049 003 1
(First edition—ISBN 0 900898 20 8)

All Scripture quotations are from the
Authorised (King James) Version

Cover photograph: © British & Foreign Bible Society
Cover design: Phil Boorman @ burgum boorman ltd

Quotations are taken from the following publications:

L Berkhof, *Systematic Theology* (Banner of Truth); Thomas Brooks, *Heaven on Earth* (Banner of Truth); E. F. Kevan, *What the Scriptures Teach* and *Now that I am a Christian* (Evangelical Press); H. R. Jones, *The Doctrine of Scripture Today* (Evangelical Press); D. M. Lloyd-Jones, Commentaries on Romans and *God's Way of Reconciliation—Ephesians 2* (Banner of Truth); Leon Morris, *The Cross in the New Testament* (Paternoster Press); J. A. Motyer, *The Tests of Faith* (Inter-Varsity Press); John Murray, *Redemption Accomplished and Applied* (Banner of Truth); C. H. Spurgeon, *Metropolitan Tabernacle Pulpit* (Banner of Truth) and *Morning and Evening* (Marshall, Morgan & Scott); A. W. Tozer, *Worship— the Missing Jewel of the Christian Church* (Christian Publications Inc.) and *Paths to Power* (Marshall, Morgan & Scott).

Published by the Bryntirion Press
Bryntirion, Bridgend CF31 4DX, Wales, UK
Printed by Creative Print & Design, Ebbw Vale

PREFACE

This booklet is intended for those who have reason to believe that they have just become Christians. It sets out to help such to understand more fully what God has done for them in salvation.

It is possible to be a Christian and not to appreciate the glory of it. Sometimes we talk of having 'accepted Jesus', or 'opened our heart to the Lord', or 'made a decision'. When we turn to the Scriptures we find that salvation is far more wonderful than these phrases imply. The Bible teaches that it is God who accepts us, not we Him (*Ephesians* 1:6); it is God who opens hearts (*Acts* 16:14); it is God who chooses us (*Ephesians* 1:4). In other words, from beginning to end, God is the author of salvation.

To benefit most from these pages they should be read carefully and slowly, and care should be taken to look up every Bible reference. God in His Word tells us of the richness of this 'so great salvation'. He wants us to know it, and to enjoy it, and to praise Him for it. So if you are a Christian, all that follows is true of you.

Scripture also warns us that it is possible to deceive ourselves— to think that we are Christians when in fact we are not (*Matthew* 7:21-23). We need to be sure and to have firm biblical grounds for our assurance. So this booklet begins with a description of a true Christian, and tells how such a person can be sure that he is a Christian, and how others can be sure also as they see Christ in him.

'If any man be in Christ, he is a new creature: old things are passed away; behold, all things are become new. And all things are of God, who hath reconciled us to himself by Jesus Christ' (*2 Corinthians* 5:17,18).

PETER JEFFERY

1
YOU ARE NOW A CHRISTIAN

You were not born a Christian.
You did not pass an exam to become a Christian.
You did not earn the right to become a Christian.
God makes a person a Christian (*Ephesians* 2:8-10; *Titus* 3:5).

To be a Christian means that
- sin, our greatest problem, has been dealt with (*1 John* 1:9)
- we are then at peace with God (*Romans* 5:1).

This God accomplishes for us in and through His Son Jesus Christ. The Christian is Christ's man. Christ is his Lord—He is not just a Saviour, but Saviour and Lord (*1 Corinthians* 6:19,20).

A Christian is complete in Christ (*Colossians* 2:10).
God's Spirit dwells in him (*1 Corinthians* 6:19,20).
He is acceptable to God through Jesus Christ (*Ephesians* 1:6).

A Christian is a child of God (*1 John* 3:1,2).
Before salvation God is not our Father (*John* 8:42-44).
Salvation means sonship. We are adopted into God's family (*Romans* 8:14-16; *Galatians* 4:4-7).

'Adoption . . . is an act of transfer from an alien family into the family of God Himself. This is surely the apex of grace and privilege . . . It staggers imagination because of its amazing condescension and love. The Spirit alone could be the seal of it in our hearts.'   *John Murray*

'Some . . . spake unto the Grecians, preaching the Lord Jesus. And the hand of the Lord was with them: and a great number believed, and turned unto the Lord . . . Barnabas . . . exhorted them all, that with purpose of heart they would cleave unto the Lord . . . And the disciples were called Christians first in Antioch' (*Acts* 11:20-23,26).

2
YOU WERE A LOST SINNER

The Bible teaches that we are all sinners (*Romans* 3:23).
We do not become sinners: we are born sinners (*Psalm* 51:5).
Sin is the natural condition of every heart (*Jeremiah* 17:9).
Many people deny this; but they are deceiving themselves
    (*1 John* 1:8,10).
Sin is the breaking of the law of God (*1 John* 3:4).

Sin brings upon man
- separation from God (*Genesis* 3:23,24; *Isaiah* 59:2)
- the wrath of God (*Romans* 1:18)
- guilt (*Romans* 3:19)
- death (*Genesis* 2:17; *Roman*s 6:23)
- hell (*Matthew* 25:41)

Death is not something reserved for the future. Before you became a
    Christian you were dead (*Ephesians* 2:1). You were dead to God;
    you did not know God, or love him, or serve him.

You were a sinner—an enemy of God.

Your condition is described in Ephesians 2:12.

In Psalm 32 you will find three different words for sin:
Transgression—this literally means 'to step over a boundary', to
    break the law of God, to go into those paths that God forbids. It is
    rebellion against God.

Sin—this means to miss the mark or target, to come short of God's
    glory (*Romans* 3:23). God sets a standard, and we fail to keep it.

Iniquity—this is a twisting, distorting perversion of the soul. Man is
    no longer as God made him. He is twisted, mis-shapen by sin.

3
HOW DID YOU BECOME
A CHRISTIAN?

You became a Christian when the Holy Spirit convicted you of sin and
- you realised your true condition (*Luke* 15:17-19)
- you repented (*Acts* 2:38)
- you believed (*Acts* 16:31)
- you received Christ (*John* 1:12)

Your conversion may have been like:

Paul's (*Acts* 9:1-22)
- from a deeply religious background
- dramatic and sudden
- saved on a particular date, at a particular place

the Philippian jailor's (*Acts* 16:23-24)
- from a very worldly background, with no previous thought for God
- circumstances brought you to despair
- not seeking God, but found by him

Timothy's (*2 Timothy* 3:15)
- brought up in a Christian home
- always known the Scriptures
- cannot say exactly when you came to faith in Jesus Christ

Lydia's (*Acts* 16:14,15)
- nothing dramatic
- seeking for a long time
- your heart quietly opened to see and believe.

How you were converted does not matter. All conversions are the work of God.

> *Some through the fire,*
> *Some through the flood,*
> *Some through the water,*
> *But all through the blood.*

4
IF YOU ARE A CHRISTIAN

● all that follows in the next pages will be true of you.

You have already been

You will now

You will need to

5
YOU HAVE BEEN CONVERTED

To convert means to change.

You have been changed (*2 Corinthians* 5:17).

You were dead: you are now alive (*Ephesians* 2:1,5).

You were lost: you are now found (*Luke* 15).

You were blind: you now see (*2 Corinthians* 4:4-6).

You were an enemy of God: you are now his child (*Romans* 5:10; 8:14-17).

The completeness of the change in the convert is clearly revealed in Ephesians 2:

verses 1-3. This is what you *were* in the sight of God.

verses 19-22. This is what you *are* in the sight of God.

The bridge between these two extreme positions is the grace of God (verses 4-18)

Note: v.1 'And you'—what you were

v. 4 'But God'—what God did for you

v.19 'Now therefore'—what you are by grace

This great work of grace becomes real to us through faith (*Ephesians* 2:8).

'What does "faith" mean? Faith includes three aspects or three elements. It means a knowledge of the truth, it means assent to truth, it means a trust in the truth. Faith, in other words, is not merely an intellectual awareness of the truth, or even an intellectual acceptance of the truth. Faith means a real trusting in Christ, and what he has done on our behalf and for our salvation.'   *D. M. Lloyd-Jones*

'Men are not saved because they turn over a new leaf. Conversion is not a meritorious action which ought to be suitably rewarded. Conversion, as the New Testament understands it, means a wholehearted turning away from sin. It means a ceasing to rely on one's own strong right arm. It means a coming to rely entirely on the mercy of God. Apart from that mercy, conversion would be aimless, futile, meaningless. Conversion roots salvation squarely in the action of God, and it takes its meaning from the action of God.'   *Leon Morris*

6
YOU HAVE BEEN BORN AGAIN

Being born again, or the new birth, or regeneration (each of these means the same thing) is the work of the Holy Spirit and it is essential (*John* 3:3-8).

Without a physical birth you cannot have physical life.
Without a spiritual birth you cannot have spiritual life.

Before you were born again, you were dead in sin. You were dead to God. You did not know him, nor understand him, nor serve him. You could not; you were spiritually dead. In the new birth the Holy Spirit gives your dead soul life (*Ezekiel* 36:26). Without this you could not believe in Christ. It is the regenerate soul alone that is able to exercise faith and receive Christ (*John* 6:44).

What can a dead man do for himself? Nothing.
What can a dead soul do for itself? Nothing.

The new birth is the work of God the Holy Spirit and him alone (*John* 3:1-12).

'Regeneration is a change which is known and felt: known by works of holiness, and felt by a gracious experience. This great work is supernatural. It is not an operation which man performs for himself: a new principle is infused, which works in the heart, renews the soul, and affects the entire man. It is not a change of my name, but a renewal of my nature, so that I am not the man I used to be, but a new man in Christ Jesus.'   *C. H. Spurgeon*

'Regeneration is the beginning of all saving grace *in us*, and all saving grace in exercise on our part proceeds from the fountain of regeneration. We are not born again by faith or repentence or conversion; we repent and believe because we have been regenerated.'   *John Murray*

7
YOU HAVE BEEN SAVED

Saved from what?
- from the consequence of your sin (*Romans* 6:23)
- from the wrath of God (*Romans* 1:18).

You needed to be saved because you were a sinner (*1 Timothy* 1:15).
Before you were saved you were lost (*Luke* 19:10; *Ephesians* 2:12).
You were guilty before God (*Romans* 3:19).

Before you could be saved
- your debt to God's law, which your sin had incurred, had to be paid (*Romans* 3:25)
- God's wrath upon your sin had to be met (*Romans* 3:25).

Many modern translations do not use the word *propitiation* in Romans 3:25. But it is essential if we are to understand the death of Christ properly. Propitiation means to turn away wrath by sacrifice.

'What the Apostle is teaching here is that what our Lord did by his death upon the cross was to appease God's wrath.'

D. M. Lloyd-Jones

'The word "propitiation" properly signifies the removal of wrath . . . it reminds us that the divine anger was exercised towards man's sin, and that it was Christ's propitiatory death that put the situation right, and made it possible for man to come back to God.'   *Leon Morris*

Jesus alone has done this when he died at Calvary in your place
(*1 Peter* 2:24; *Romans* 5:6).

There is only one Saviour (*Acts* 4:12).
There is only one way to God (*John* 14:6).
There is only one mediator (*1 Timothy* 2:5).

Jesus is God's provision to deal with sin (*Matthew* 1:21).

8
YOU HAVE BEEN FORGIVEN

All sin is against God (*Psalm* 51:4).
Sin breaks the law of God (*1 John* 3:4).
Therefore only God can forgive sin (*Luke* 23:34).
God delights to forgive (*Psalm* 86:5).

Because Jesus died in our place and paid the full penalty of sin,
God is now able to forgive us justly (*1 John* 1:9).

God forgives us through Jesus Christ, who
- died to purchase forgiveness for us (*Ephesians* 1:7)
- arose from the dead to give us forgiveness (*Acts* 5:31).

In Christ your sin is forgiven (*1 John* 2:12).
- it is blotted out (*Isaiah* 44:22)
- God remembers it no more (*Jeremiah* 31:34)
- it is removed from you (*Psalm* 103:12).

> *Pardon—from an offended God!*
> *Pardon—for sins of deepest dye!*
> *Pardon—bestowed through Jesus' blood!*
> *Pardon—that brings the rebel nigh!*
>
> *Who is a pardoning God like Thee?*
> *Or who has grace so rich and free?*

'It is our unspeakable comfort, in all our approaches to God, that there is forgiveness in him, for that is what we need. He has put himself into a capacity to pardon sin, he has declared himself gracious and merciful, and ready to forgive (*Exodus* 34:6,7). He has promised to forgive the sins of those that do repent. Never any that dealt with him found him implacable, but easy to be entreated and swift to show mercy. With us there is iniquity, and therefore it is well for us that with him there is forgiveness.'   *Matthew Henry*

> *In wonder lost, with trembling joy,*
> *We take the pardon of our God,*
> *Pardon for sins of deepest dye,*
> *A pardon sealed with Jesus' blood.*

9
YOU HAVE BEEN RECONCILED

Reconciliation means to remove the enmity or quarrel between two people and bring them together in peace.

On four occasions the New Testament speaks of the work and ministry of Christ in terms of reconciliation (*Romans* 5:10; *Ephesians* 2:16; *Colossians* 1:21; *2 Corinthians* 5:18-21).

In reconciliation God deals with our sin and brings us to himself in peace and as his redeemed children. All this God accomplishes in Christ.

How does he do it? Read again 2 Corinthians 5:18-21.

- God does not impute, put our sin to our account. He cancels the debt we have incurred by breaking his law (v.19).
- Our sin is imputed to (put to the account of) Jesus (v.21a).
- The punishment our sin deserves is poured out upon the Lord Jesus Christ. Jesus pays the debt. He is treated as the sinner should be, and he dies (*Isaiah* 53:5).
- The righteousness of Jesus is put to our account (v.21b). We are treated as children of God, joint heirs with Christ (*Romans* 8:17).

Having been reconciled, you now have access to God (*Ephesians* 2:16-18).

'Reconciliation is amazing. But this is more wondrous and more amazing. Reconciliation is not the end. Beyond reconciliation we have access to the Father . . . My friends, this is the grand end and object of salvation, that we enter into the presence of God and have fellowship with him. We are no longer afar off, we have been made nigh, we are brought right in, we are face to face with him, we have fellowship with God. To know God and Jesus Christ whom he has sent. Have you got the access, have you realised it? Are you exercising your right to it?'   *D. M. Lloyd-Jones*

10
YOU HAVE BEEN JUSTIFIED

Justification is a legal term.
It is the opposite of condemnation (*Romans* 8:33,34).

Justification is the sovereign work of God whereby he declares the sinner to be righteous, and the rightful demands of the law satisfied.

God's law condemns the sinner.
God's love and grace justify the sinner (*Romans* 3:24).

Justification is not earned by man (*Galatians* 2:16).

God justifies on the basis of the righteousness of Jesus Christ and his atoning death for sinners (*Romans* 5:8,9).

Justification removes the guilt of sin (*Romans* 8:1).

Justification imputes (credits, puts to our account) to the sinner the righteousness of Christ (*Romans* 4:20-25).

Justification is once and for all. There are no degrees of justification. You are as justified now as you ever shall be, and as justified as any other Christian.

'Justification does not *make* the sinner any different: it *declares* him just in the eyes of the law. The sinner certainly needs to be *made* good, and the Holy Spirit will go on to do that in what is known as "sanctification": but let us be clear in our minds about justification first. Justification has to do not with our *state*, but with our *standing*: it refers to our position before God. Apart from Christ we have no standing at all; we are guilty and condemned: but with Christ as our Saviour and substitute we are acquitted and justified, for he has borne our sin himself. You will find all this put very clearly in Romans 3:23-26.'
E. F. Kevan

11
THROUGH FAITH

Justification comes to us through faith (*Romans* 5:1).

We are not justified because of faith, or on account of our faith. We are justified THROUGH faith. Faith is the channel by which the righteousness of God comes to us (*Ephesians* 2:8).

Where does faith come from?
- It is a gift of God (*Ephesians* 2:8).
- It comes by hearing the gospel (*Romans* 10:17).

Faith is not blind. It is belief in Christ (*Acts* 20:21; *Ephesians* 1:15).
It is belief in who he is, and what he alone is able to do (*Matthew* 8:5-10).
Faith incorporates trust and belief (*Romans* 4:20,21).

In faith we receive Christ (*John* 1:12).

'Faith in Jesus Christ is a saving grace, whereby we receive and rest upon him alone for salvation, as he is offered to us in the gospel.'   *Shorter Catechism*

'Paul does not see faith as a mere intellectual adherence to certain doctrines. Faith for Paul is a warm personal trust in a living Saviour. Faith is a transforming attitude. When a man believes, his whole personality is affected. The entire Christian life accordingly is a life of faith, or, as Paul puts it, "we walk by faith, not by sight" (*2 Corinthians* 5:7).'   *Leon Morris*

David Dickson, once Professor of Divinity in Edinburgh, being asked, when on his deathbed, how he found himself, answered, 'I have taken my good deeds and bad deeds, and thrown them together in a heap, and fled from them both to Christ, and in him I have peace.'

12
YOU HAVE BEEN JOINED
TO CHRIST

One of the most glorious features of salvation is that we now have
union with Christ.

Before we were saved, we were 'without Christ' (*Ephesians* 2:12).

Now we are 'in Christ' (*Ephesians* 1:1).

The Apostle Paul delighted to speak of being 'in Christ'. He uses the
phrase nine or more times in Ephesians 1:1-14.

What does it mean to be 'in Christ'?

- It means that Christ is our Head, our Representative. In Adam
  we were guilty and condemned: in Christ we are justified and
  pardoned (*Romans* 5:12-21).
- It means that we have a living, vital, organic union with Christ
  (*John* 15:4,5).

In Christ

- we have all spiritual blessings (*Ephesians* 1:3)
- we are chosen (*Ephesians* 1:4)
- we are loved by God (*Romans* 8:39)
- we are brought nigh to God (*Ephesians* 2:13)
- we are complete (*Colossians* 2:10)
- we are created anew (*Ephesians* 2:10)
- we are all one (*Galatians* 3:28)
- even death cannot sever this union (*1 Thessalonians* 4:14-16).

'All these blessings that we enjoy become ours because we are
joined to Christ. We can therefore claim that what has happened to
Christ has happened to us. This is the marvel and the mystery of our
salvation . . . The Son of God came down from heaven to earth; he
took upon him human nature, he joined human nature unto himself,
he shared human nature; and as the result of his work we human
beings share his life and are in him, and are participators in all the
benefits that come from him.'   *D. M. Lloyd-Jones*

13
ASSURANCE

God wants you to be sure of your salvation (*Hebrews* 10:22).

Assurance comes through the Scriptures (*1 John* 5:13).
Assurance comes through the Holy Spirit *(Romans* 8:16).

The Scriptures tell you that if you are a Christian you will

- love righteousness and hate sin (*John* 3:20,21)
- love other Christians (*1 John* 3:14)
- love the things of God (*1 John* 2:3-5)
- love the Lord Jesus Christ (*1 Peter* 2:7)
- want to see others saved (*Romans* 10:1).

Being a Christian does not mean that you are sinless (*1 John* 1:8-10). You will still sin, but the difference now is that you will hate it and daily seek God's forgiveness (*Psalm* 51).

If these things are true of you, no matter how faintly, these are the marks of grace. You are being led by the Holy Spirit *(Romans* 8:14).

The Holy Spirit witnesses inwardly (*Romans* 8:16).

This the Spirit does by telling us directly and giving us experiences of God's great love to us *(Romans* 5:5).

It is the Holy Spirit who enables us to discern the marks of grace, and who pours into our hearts God's fatherly love.

You can be a Christian without having assurance. But God wants you to have assurance, so pray earnestly for it. Be satisfied with nothing less than full assurance. Do not let Satan rob you of this.

'Such is Satan's envy and enmity against a Christian's joy and comfort, that he cannot but act to the utmost of his line to keep poor souls in doubt and darkness. Satan knows . . . that assurance is that which will make men strong to do exploits, to shake his tottering kingdom about his ears; and therefore he is very studious and industrious to keep souls off from assurance, as he was to cast Adam out of paradise.' *Thomas Brooks*

14
YOU CANNOT LOSE YOUR SALVATION

You are now beginning to appreciate something of the wonder of what God has done for you. But is it too good to last? Take heart, read John 10:28,29.

You cannot lose your salvation because

- Christ has given you ETERNAL life.
- Christ has said you shall NEVER perish.
- you are held in the hand of ALMIGHTY GOD.
- you have been GIVEN by God the Father to Jesus.

In other words, God has saved you, and not you yourself (John 6:37,44,65).

God began the work of salvation; God will complete it (*Philippians* 1:6).

Read Psalm 23, and note that because the Lord is your Shepherd certain other things follow as a consequence. All lead to the great climax: 'and I will dwell in the house of the Lord FOR EVER.'

Praise God for the truth of Psalm 37:23-29.

> *What from Christ that soul shall sever,*
> *Bound by everlasting bands?*
> *Once in Him, in Him for ever,*
> *Thus the eternal covenant stands:*
> *None shall pluck thee*
> *From the Strength of Israel's hands.*

'For I am persuaded that neither death, nor life, nor angels, nor principalities, nor powers, nor things present, nor things to come, nor height, nor depth, nor any other creature, shall be able to separate us from the love of God, which is in Christ Jesus our Lord' (*Romans* 8:38,39).

15
BELONGING TO A CHURCH

The word 'church' is used in Scripture in two ways:
- the whole church, at all times, in all places (*Colossians* 1:18)
- the local church, at a particular place (*1 Corinthians* 1:2).

When you are converted you become a member of the true church, the body of Christ. But you need also to link up with a local church. Why?
- because you need the teaching and ministry (*Acts* 2:42)
- because you need the fellowship (*Acts* 2:42-46).

You may find help and encouragement from Christian groups outside the church, e.g. Christian organisations at school, university or work. These are good, but they are not a substitute for the church. The church is not instituted by man, but is God's provision for his people (*Ephesians* 5:25; 4:11-12).

A Christian should belong to a local church—worship there, work there, have fellowship there. This does not mean he never goes to any other church, but he 'belongs' in one place. If this does not take place, then the following scriptures are impossible to fulfil—*Hebrews* 13:17; *Acts* 14:23; *Acts* 6:3; *Hebrews* 10:24,25.

Do not be what Spurgeon called 'birds of passage which nest nowhere'. Do not drift from church to church. Belong!

Which church? Unfortunately, today, all churches are not alike. You need a church that will help you grow as a Christian. You need a church that is seeking to order its life and ministry according to Scripture. You never find in New Testament churches whist drives, jumble sales or dances.

You do find
- Bible teaching (*Acts* 2:42)
- prayer meetings (*Acts* 4:23-31)
- evangelism (*Acts* 11:20,21).

Find a good church. Worship there. Become a member there. Pray for its ministry. Make your friends there. Take your friends there.

16
WORSHIP

'Worship is to feel in the heart a humbling but delightful sense of admiring awe and astonished wonder, and to express it in some appropriate manner. Worship is awesome wonder and overpowering love in the presence of God.'   *A. W. Tozer*

All Christians go to church every Sunday if at all possible.

We go to church to worship God
- because of God's command (*Hebrews* 10:25)
- because of Christ's example (*Luke* 4:16)
- because we want to go (*Psalm* 122:1).

Worship is the chief end of man. Man was created to worship God. Sin made that impossible. But your sin has been dealt with. You can now enjoy the greatest privilege known to man. You can worship God. There is no substitute for worship. It is the highest delight of heaven and earth.

We worship God
- because of who he is (*Psalm* 99:5; 96:8,9)
- because of what he has done for us (*Revelation* 5:11-14).

Worship is, of course, not confined to a building, or to a Sunday. It is the continual privilege of the people of God.

'What are the factors that you will find present in worship?
- *Boundless confidence*—you cannot worship a Being you cannot trust *(Hebrews* 4:14-16)
- *Admiration*—appreciation of the excellency of God (*Psalm* 8)
- *Fascination*—entranced with who God is: the magnitude and splendour of Almighty God (*Isaiah* 40)
- *Adoration*—to love God with all the power within us (*Psalm* 116).'   *A. W. Tozer*

17
HEARING THE WORD PREACHED

The preaching and exposition of Scripture is the God-ordained means
- for spreading the gospel (*1 Corinthians* 1:21)
- for instructing his people (*Acts* 2:42; *2 Timothy* 4:2; 1:11).

To hear the Word preached is not enough (*Hebrews* 4:2).
If it is to profit you
- you must listen (*Mark* 4:14)
- you must obey (*Luke* 8:21; *Psalm* 119:9).

How can you get the most out of a sermon?
- Follow the preaching with an open Bible (*Acts* 8:27-35)
- Listen to a man who expounds the Bible (*Nehemiah* 8:8)
- Have a due reverence for the Word (*Nehemiah* 8:5)
- Listen attentively (*Nehemiah* 8:3)
- Let the Word deal with you (*Nehemiah* 8:9)
- Do not be too occupied with your watch (*Nehemiah* 8:3)
- If you do not understand, ask afterwards (*Acts* 8:34)

Pray for those who preach the Word (*Ephesians* 6:19).
Pray that they may have the Holy Spirit's power and authority
(*1 Thessalonians* 1:5; *1 Corinthians* 2:4).
Pray for the success of the Word (*Acts* 4:29,30).

'I warn then everyone who loves his soul to be jealous as to the preaching he regularly hears and the place of worship he regularly attends. He who deliberately settles down under a ministry which is unsound is a very unwise man. If false doctrine is preached in a church a man who loves his soul is not right in going to that church.'   *J . C . Ryle*

'The most urgent need in the Christian Church today is true preaching: and as it is the greatest and most urgent need in the Church, it is obviously the greatest need of the world also.'   *D . M . Lloyd-Jones*

18
THE LORD'S SUPPER

There are two 'sacraments'. The word sacrament means a sacred sign. These are symbolical rites in which the spiritual meaning of our salvation is enshrined. The 'word' preaches to the ear, and the 'sacrament' preaches to the eye. The two sacraments are (a) the Lord's Supper, and (b) Baptism.

The Lord's Supper is given three names in the New Testament:
- the breaking of bread (*Acts* 2:42)
- the communion (*1 Corinthians 1*0:16)
- the Lord's Supper (*1 Corinthians* 11:20).

It was instituted by Jesus (*Matthew* 26:26-28).
Paul teaches about it (*1 Corinthians* 11:23-25).

The bread and wine symbolise the broken body and shed blood of Jesus. They do not turn into the body and blood: they represent it. The Lord's Supper is not a sacrifice: it reminds us of what Christ has already done (*1 Corinthians* 11:24,25).

- It proclaims his death *(1 Corinthians* 11:26).
- It points to a new covenant (*Matthew* 26:28).
- It declares the unity of all Christians (*1 Corinthians* 10:16,17).
- It is to be held regularly (*Acts* 2:46).
- It is to be held until Christ comes again (*1 Corinthians* 11:26).

'The Lord's Supper is a sacrament, wherein, by giving and receiving bread and wine, according to Christ's appointment, his death is showed forth; and the worthy receivers are, not after a corporal and carnal manner, but by faith, made partakers of his body and blood, with all his benefits, to their spiritual nourishment, and growth in grace.'   *Shorter Catechism*

19
BAPTISM

Jesus never baptised anyone. But he was baptised himself (*Matthew* 3:13-17) and he did command his disciples to baptise (*Matthew* 28:19; *Mark* 16:16).

Baptism symbolises
- union with Christ in his death, burial and resurrection (*Romans* 6:4-6)
- the washing away of our sin (*Acts* 22:16).

Christians differ on the question of baptism:
- **Some Christians** believe that the infant children of believers are eligible. They hold that the covenant God made with Abraham is a spiritual covenant, and that circumcision was the sign and seal of this. Infants shared in the benefits of the covenant and so received the sign and seal.

  Therefore, they believe, the children of believers should be baptised. See Colossians 2:11,12. This baptism is usually administered by sprinkling water on the infant.

  'In the new dispensation baptism is by divine authority substituted for circumcision as the initiatory sign and seal of the covenant of grace.'   *Berkhof*
- **Other Christians** believe that baptism must follow conversion because in the New Testament it always followed conversion (*Acts* 8:36-38; 9:17,18; 16:31-33), and was administered only to those who had repented of their sin and come to trust and believe in Christ (*Acts* 2:37-41).

  This baptism is therefore known as 'believers' baptism'. It is usually administered by immersion in water, in the belief that this alone fulfils the symbolism of baptism, and that the word *baptise* means to dip or immerse.

Baptism is not essential to salvation. But because Christ commands it, it is essential to obedience.

This is not the place to argue the differences. There are many books you can read on the subject, but, more importantly, consult your pastor, or the elders/deacons of your church.

20
LIVING THE CHRISTIAN LIFE

Your new faith must show in your life.

Good works do not save (*Ephesians* 2:8,9), but they are important.
They are the fruit of salvation (*James* 2:17; *Ephesians* 2:10).
You will not be sinless and perfect this side of heaven, but you are
    already indwelt by the Lord Jesus Christ (*Colossians* 1:27;
    Romans 8:10; *John* 15:4).
Christ must be seen in you. How is this possible? Read Romans 12:1,2.

Your main desire now will be to please God (*1 Corinthians*
    10:31).
Your standard of behaviour is now the Bible (*Psalm* 119:9,105).

The world's standards are so different from God's standards that
    many people will not understand your new life (*1 Peter* 4:3,4).
For example, see what the Christian's attitude is towards
- work and employers (*Ephesians* 6:5-7)
- authority (*Romans* 13:1-7)
- sex (*Matthew* 5:27,28).

God is pleased and glorified when Christians
- think of others less fortunate than themselves (*James* 1:27)
- use their talents to help others (*Acts* 9:36,39).
Read also Matthew 5–8 and Ephesians 4–6.

Such a life needs two things
- the enabling power of the Holy Spirit (*Romans* 8:9-14)
- faithfulness on your part (*Matthew* 25:21).

You are not faithful by being indifferent, or casual, or half-hearted.
    You must be determined. You must purpose in your heart (*Daniel*
    1:8).

Thus will God be glorified in your life (*Matthew* 5:16).

21
BIBLE STUDY (1)

The Bible is a unique book

It is not the word of man (*2 Peter* 1:20,21).
It is inspired by God (*2 Timothy* 3:16,17).

All Christians need to feed on God's Word daily (*Matthew* 4:4).
New Christians need this especially (*1 Peter* 2:2).

There are many Bible-reading schemes available today, and they will certainly help you as a new Christian (see page 29). There are also many excellent commentaries on the books of the Bible. But seek advice from more experienced Christians before you buy any.

Do not confuse Bible reading with Bible study. Merely reading a dozen or so verses a day is not enough. You need to give time and thought to the Word (*2 Timothy* 2:15; *Psalm* 119:15).
Endeavour to memorise portions of Scripture (*Psalm* 119:11).

'Be prayerful in your readings, but do not think that "prayerful" means "magical", and that something mysterious is going to "happen" when you read. God's book has to be studied intelligently and will give its truth to the thoughtful mind.' *E. F. Kevan*

'We ought not to measure, censure and understand the Scriptures according to our own natural sense and reason, but we ought diligently by prayer to meditate therein and to search after the same. The Holy Ghost must be the only master to teach us, and let youth and scholar not be ashamed to learn of this tutor.' *Martin Luther*

'For as God alone can properly bear witness to his own words, so these words will not obtain full credit in the hearts of men, until they are sealed by the inward testimony of the Spirit . . .' *John Calvin*

22
BIBLE STUDY (2)

Bible study should always commence with prayer for the illumination of the Holy Spirit, without whose help we cannot rightly understand the truths that God would have us believe.

The words of Scripture should always be taken in the sense that the writer intended, and therefore in order to interpret Scripture aright we must pay attention to its plain meaning and grammatical construction. Only by doing so can we give evidence of our belief in the Scripture's claim to verbal inspiration and hope to profit thereby.

We must never attempt to interpret a word, sentence, verse or paragraph except in terms of its context.

The infallible rule of the interpretation of Scripture is the Scripture itself. Each passage of Scripture must therefore be interpreted in the light of the rest of Scripture, and difficult passages in the light of plainer, clearer passages. We should always remember that, whereas the rule is infallible, our interpretation of it is not.

God does not give us light on everything at once. Unresolved difficulties should not be allowed to hinder the consecutive study of the Word of God. Make a note of problems that arise in the course of study, consult commentaries, and ask help of older Christians and ministers on these matters.

Bible study cannot be divorced from conduct. God will give us increased light only as we walk in the light we have been given.

'The Bible is a book which, though it is written by men for men, is yet written by God for his own glory. Its subject matter is God, and how he becomes *our* God through Jesus Christ . . . It is therefore a book which must be studied in its own light, and that is the light shed on the words by its Author—God, the Holy Spirit.'
Hywel R. Jones

23
PRAYER

Worship is more than a weekly activity in church (*Daniel* 6:10).

Daily, private prayer is your privilege (*Luke* 18:1; 11:1-13).
See the example of Jesus (*Luke* 6:12; *Matthew* 14:23; *Mark* 1:35).

'Prayer is an offering up of our desires unto God, for things agreeable to his will, in the name of Christ, with confession of our sins, and thankful acknowledgement of his mercies.'
Shorter Catechism

Prayer is to be
- regular (*Colossians* 4:2)
- fervent (*James* 5:16)
- for yourself (*Matthew* 6:9-13)
- for others (*Colossians* 1:9)
- expectant (*Mark* 11:24)
- persistent (*Luke* 11:5-8)
- with humility and penitence (*Luke* 18:13,14).

'God by his Holy Spirit approaches us in the secret place of our hearts and then, by that same Holy Spirit, He creates desires in us for himself. Our new life is a life that comes from God and so needs to sustain itself by God. We cannot therefore have the life of God within us without the experience of prayer.'   *E. F. Kevan*

It is good to have a special time every day to meet with God. Some Christians prefer the early morning, others the evening. Find a convenient time for yourself.

Jesus in Matthew 6:6 shows us the value of private prayer. But we are also encouraged to meet together for prayer (*Matthew* 18:19,20).

The Christians in Acts met often to pray (*Acts* 1:14; 2:42; 4:24-31; 12:5).

24
WITNESS

Having received so great salvation, there is an obligation upon Christians to tell others of the gospel.

We tell others of the love of God because
- Jesus commands it (*Acts* 1:8; *Mark* 5:19)
- we cannot but tell (*2 Corinthians* 5:14; *John* 15:27)
- we fear for lost souls (*2 Corinthians* 5:11).

The Holy Spirit witnesses and convicts men. This is his work (*John* 16:8-11; *1 John* 5:6,9). But he uses us, and provides opportunities for us to tell people of the love of God.

We witness in various ways by
- telling of our experience of Christ (*John* 4:29,30)
- explaining Scripture (*Acts* 8:26-35)
- inviting people to hear the gospel preached (*Acts* 10:24; *Luke* 5:29)
- the quality of our life (*Matthew* 5:16).

The witness of our lips must be backed up by the witness of our behaviour. People will dismiss all that we say if they do not see the gospel having an effect upon our lives. This is particularly true of relatives and workmates.

Be concerned for individuals.

'If you had one hundred empty bottles before you, and threw a pail of water over them, some would get a little in them, but most would fall outside. If you wish to fill the bottles, the best way is to take each bottle separately and put a vessel full of water to the bottle's mouth. That is successful personal work.'　　　*C. H. Spurgeon*

> *My gracious Master and my God,*
> *Assist me to proclaim,*
> *To spread through all the earth abroad*
> *The honours of Thy name.*

25
OBEYING GOD

'To obey, in the New Testament usage, means to give earnest attention to the Word, to submit to its authority, and to carry out its instructions.'
A. W. Tozer

Jesus himself gives a prominence to obedience that we dare not ignore, both in his example and teaching.

To Christ
- obedience was a delight (*John* 4:34)
- obedience was absolute (*Philippians* 2:8).

Obedience is essential
- to blessing (*Exodus* 19:5)
- to belonging to Christ (*Mark* 3:35)
- to abiding in Christ (*John* 15:10)
- as proof of salvation (*1 John* 2:3-5).

Do not wait to be 'convicted' about things: if God has commanded something, do it.

Peter opens his first epistle by telling us that we are 'elected . . . unto obedience' (*1 Peter* 1:2). In verse 14 he comes back to it. There it is again in verse 22. Obedience is the starting-point of the sanctified life.

There is no substitute for obedience (*1 Samuel* 15:22).

Obedience ought not to be a cold, mechanical thing. It should stem from love for God and communion with him. Communion and obedience are twins. We are rarely told in Scripture to obey the commands of God: we are told rather—'obey me', 'obey my voice' (*Exodus* 19:5; *Joshua* 24:24; *Jeremiah* 7:23; *Hebrews* 5:9).

'The Bible recognises no faith that does not lead to obedience, nor does it recognise any obedience that does not spring from faith. The two are opposite sides of the same coin. So faith and obedience are for ever joined and each is without value when separated from the other. The trouble with many of us today is that we are trying to believe without intending to obey.'
A . W. Tozer

26
TEMPTATIONS AND TRIALS

You are now a Christian, and yet sin troubles you more than it did before your conversion. You are more aware of sin now than you ever were (*Romans* 7:21-25).

Temptation is not a sin. To all Christians it is a very real problem.
Christ was tempted (*Luke* 4:1-13).

'Do not suppose that it is only the worldly-minded who have dreadful thoughts and blasphemous temptations, for even spiritual-minded persons endure the same: and in the holiest position we may suffer the darkest temptation.' *C. H. Spurgeon*

Memorise 1 Corinthians 10:13
Temptation comes to all Christians—'common to man'
Temptation is not compulsion—'not tempted above that ye are able'
You can say Yes or No—God gives 'a way of escape'.

There is a difference between trials and temptations.
The devil tempts you to sin—to disobey God (*2 Corinthians* 11:3).

But the Devil cannot make you sin.
He could when you were his slave (*Romans* 6:16)
Christ is now your Lord (*Romans* 6:17,18)
The Devil has no claim on you (*Romans* 6:6, 11-14).

God sends trials to test his people (*Genesis* 22:1; *1 Peter* 1:6,7).

'The trials are not unnatural things, nor obstacles to spiritual growth. They are God's appointed way forward.' *J. A. Motyer*

When tempted or tried
- believe that God is faithful and look for the way of escape (*1 Corinthians* 10:13)
- resist (*James* 4:7)
- endure and triumph (*James* 1:12)
- turn the temptation into blessing (*James* 1:2-4)
- learn from Luke 4 how Jesus dealt with temptation—he answered with Scripture (vv.4,8,12).

27
THE DEVIL

Is the Devil fact or fiction?

It used to be fashionable not to believe in the Devil. People made him out to be a comic figure of mythology in red tights, with horns and a tail. But the Bible knows better. The devil is real—as real as God.

The Devil was once an angel who rebelled against God (*Isaiah* 14:12-20).

His continual work is to oppose God and God's people (*Luke* 22:31,32; *1 Thessalonians* 2:18; *Matthew* 4:1).

This opposition is sometimes fierce and obvious. He comes at us like a 'roaring lion' (*1 Peter* 5:8).

At other times he is more devious, and comes as an 'angel of light' (*2 Corinthians* 11:14).

This second ploy is perhaps the more dangerous. Paul warns us of the 'wiles of the devil' (*Ephesians* 6:11).

The Bible continually warns us of the Devil's cunning. Note the following terms: • 'more subtle' (*Genesis* 3:1); • 'his devices' (*2 Corinthians* 2:11); • 'a liar' (*John* 8:44); • he 'beguiled Eve' (*2 Corinthians* 11:3); • 'the snare of the devil' (*1 Timothy* 3:7); • he 'deceiveth the whole world' (*Revelation* 12:9).

The moment you become a Christian all these wiles are used against you. Never minimise the power of the Devil, but do not exaggerate it either. He is mighty, but not almighty. The Almighty God, our Father and Saviour, has given us the means to defeat the Devil (*Ephesians* 6:10-20).

Before conversion you were the servant of the Devil (*John* 8:44; *Ephesians* 2:2,3; *1 John* 5:19).

The Devil is the prince of the world (*John* 12:31).
On the cross Jesus defeated the devil (*Colossians* 2:14,15).

You can defeat him too, but only in Christ.
Read James 4:7 and note that you can only resist the Devil effectively when you are first submitted to God.

28
ENJOYING GOD

Christianity was never meant to make your life drab and miserable.

You are meant to have
- abundance of life (*John* 10:10)
- joy (*1 Peter* 1:8)
- peace (*Romans* 5:1)
- contentment (*Philippians* 4:11).

If all that we have dealt with so far is true, then this joy and peace should also be true of you.

If you are to enjoy God, to enjoy your new Christian life, there is only one way (*Philippians* 4:4-9). The way to enjoy God is to give yourself to God (*Romans* 12:1,2).

The half-hearted, compromising Christian is always miserable (*Mark* 14:66-72).

The dedicated Christian can rejoice even in troubles (*Acts* 5:40,41).

You have much to rejoice in:
- the incomparable privilege of being a Christian (*Philippians* 3:7-9)
- God's love to you as an individual (*Galatians* 2:20)
- God's promise to keep you (*2 Corinthians* 4:6-18)
- your inheritance (*1 Peter* 1:3-9).

You cannot enjoy God from a distance. You need to get close to him (*Psalm* 16:11).

All the gifts of God are for us to enjoy, but the greatest pleasure is to enjoy God himself.

'Thank God for little grace, and ask him for great grace. He has given thee hope, ask for faith: and when he gives thee faith, ask for assurance: and when thou gettest assurance, ask for full assurance; and when thou hast obtained full assurance, ask for enjoyment: and when thou hast enjoyment, ask for glory itself: and he shall surely give it thee in his own appointed season.'   *C. H . Spurgeon*

BIBLE READING AIDS

- A new Christian needs to learn to appreciate the Bible and two books that would greatly help in this are: *How to Enjoy Your Bible* by John Blanchard; *Handle with Care* by Sinclair Ferguson.

- Start your study of the Bible in the New Testament. To help you appreciate each book of the New Testament read: *Stepping Stones* by Peter Jeffery which is a New Testament guide for beginners.

- Going on with God depends, among other things, on your daily reading and study of the Bible. Most Christians find that daily reading notes can be a great help. A good place to start is in Mark's Gospel, using the notes by John Blanchard entitled *Read, Mark, Learn* (Evangelical Press).

- There are many daily Bible reading notes available. One of the best is Geneva Bible Notes, obtainable from Grace Publications Trust, The Christian Bookshop, Sevenoaks Road, Pratts Bottom, Orpington BR6 7SQ.

- For Welsh-speaking readers, a series of Bible-study booklets entitled *Bara'r Bywyd*, each with sufficient daily readings for two months, is published by Bryntirion Press.

- Other useful aids for Bible study are: *Searching the Word: A Method for the Personal Study of the Scriptures* (Bryntirion Press); *M'Cheyne's Calendar for Daily Readings*—a reading plan covering the whole Bible in one year (Banner of Truth); *Reading the Bible* by Geoffrey Thomas—a booklet with much helpful advice and a daily reading plan covering the Bible in a year (Banner of Truth); *Firm Foundations* by Peter Jeffery & Owen Milton—a two-month Bible reading course introducing the reader to some great chapters of the Bible (Bryntirion Press).

- It is a good idea to build up a small collection of reference books to aid your Bible study. The following would help you for many years: *The New Bible Dictionary* (Inter-Varsity Press); a good Bible concordance; *The Lion Handbook to the Bible* (Lion Publishing).

SUGGESTED FURTHER READING

Right With God by John Blanchard; *Now that I am a Christian* by E. F. Kevan; *Walk Worthy* by Peter Jeffery; *Learning and Living* by John Blanchard; *Add to your Faith* by Sinclair B. Ferguson.

Biographies that between them give you an introduction to the lives of a number of Christians: *God Made Them Great* by John Tallach; *The Young Spurgeon* by Peter Jeffery; *God's Outlaw* by Brian H. Edwards.

Christian Handbook by Peter Jeffery is a straightforward guide to the Bible, church history and Christian doctrine. It provides in one handy volume a wide range of information which would otherwise only be found in much larger and more expensive volumes.